# PASSPORT
# HONG KONG

# Passport to the World

Passport Argentina
Passport Brazil
Passport China
Passport France
Passport Germany
Passport India
Passport Indonesia
Passport Israel
Passport Italy
Passport Japan
Passport Korea
Passport Malaysia
Passport Mexico
Passport Russia
Passport Singapore
Passport South Africa
Passport Spain
Passport Taiwan
Passport Thailand
Passport United Kingdom
Passport USA
Passport Vietnam

# PASSPORT
# HONG KONG

Your Pocket Guide
to
Hong Kong Business,
Customs & Etiquette

Andrew Grzeskowiak

Passport Series Editor: Barbara Szerlip

**WORLD TRADE PRESS®**
*Professional Books for International Trade*

World Trade Press
1505 Fifth Avenue
San Rafael, California 94901
Tel: (415) 454-9934
Fax: (415) 453-7980
USA Order Line: (800) 833-8586
E-mail: WorldPress@aol.com

"Passport to the World" concept: Edward Hinkelman
Cover design: Peter Jones
Illustrations: Tom Watson

Copyright ©1996 by World Trade Press. All rights reserved.

Reproduction of any part of this work beyond that permitted by Section 107 or 108 of the United States Copyright Act without the express written permission of the copyright holder is unlawful. Requests for permission or further information should be addressed to World Trade Press at the address above.

This publication is designed to provide general information concerning the cultural aspects of doing business with people from a particular country. It is sold with the understanding that the publisher is not engaged in rendering legal or any other professional services. If legal advice or other expert assistance is required, the services of a competent professional person should be sought.

Library of Congress Cataloging-in-Publication Data
Grzeskowiak, Andrew, 1947-
Passport Hong Kong: your pocket guide to Hong Kong business, customs & etiquette / Andrew Grzeskowiak.
p. cm. -- ("Passport to the World")
Includes bibliographical references (p. 93)
ISBN 1-885073-31-3
1. Corporate culture -- Hong Kong. 2. Business etiquette -- Hong Kong. 3. Industrial management--Social aspects--Hong Kong. 4. Negotiation in business -- Hong Kong. 5. Intercultural communication. I. series.
HD58.7.G79 1996
390' .0095125--dc20
96-14868
CIP

Printed in the United States of America

# Table of Contents
# Hong Kong
*The Fragrant Harbor*

## Overview

1: Doing Business Across Cultures ...... 6
    Hong Kong Quick Look ............... 10
2: Country Facts .................... 11
3: The People of Hong Kong ............ 14
4: Cultural Stereotypes ................ 21
5: Regional Differences ................ 25

## Business Environment

6: Government & Business .............. 27
7: The Work Environment .............. 30
8: Women in Business ................. 36
9: Making Connections ................ 39
10: Strategies for Success .............. 41
11: Time ............................ 46
12: Business Meetings ................. 49
13: Negotiating with Hong Kong Chinese ..... 52
14: Business Outside the Law ........... 61

## Customs & Etiquette

15: Names & Greetings ................ 64
16: Communication Styles .............. 68
17: Customs ......................... 72
18: Dress & Appearance ............... 76
19: Reading the Hong Kong Chinese ...... 78
20: Entertaining: The Banquet Tradition ... 80
21: Socializing ....................... 86

## Additional Information

22: Basic Cantonese Phrases ........... 90
23: Correspondence ................... 91
24: Useful Numbers ................... 92
25: Books & Internet Addresses ......... 93

# 1. Doing Business Across Cultures

The past decade has seen a dramatic lowering of trade barriers, the globalization of markets, and explosive growth in international trade. The business world has become increasingly interdependent, creating both new challenges and exciting new opportunities.

In order to conduct business abroad, you need to understand the environment in which your foreign counterparts operate. You will probably never know a particular culture as well as your own — not only is the language different, but the historical and cultural context within which its people operate is often misunderstood by outsiders.

But even a little bit of knowledge can help you develop closer, more successful relationships with your associates. And your international transactions will be far more enjoyable as a result.

## Think Globally, Act Locally

Although business operations have become highly internationalized, national and local traditions, attitudes and beliefs remain diverse. Everyone's perceptions — what we see, hear, taste, touch and smell — are filtered through a particular set of beliefs and assumptions.

When you understand that your own cultural background colors your world view, you can begin to appreciate that your foreign associate may have an entirely different perspective, and that he or she may approach a situation in a totally different and unexpected way.

For example, whereas Westerners tend to value individuality of thought and action, Eastern cultures prize conformity and harmony of purpose. While an Englishman's primary focus may be to conclude the business at hand, a Hong Kong Chinese will concentrate on first developing a personal relationship. Public praise is much enjoyed by North Americans, but it is a source of embarrassment and discomfort for Japanese and Chinese. Failure to recognize these inherent differences will result in misconceptions and inappropriate responses that can doom a business relationship.

## The Cross-Cultural Key

Cross-cultural understanding is crucial if you wish to develop personal relationships that will lead to business success abroad. Such an understanding will allow you to recognize important hints and undercurrents that can have a profound effect on the outcome of your transactions.

For example, silence at a negotiating table can signify a number of different things. In Japan, silence might mean that your counterparts are seriously considering what has just been said, or it might be a bargaining ploy. In the USA, it usually signals a great deal of discomfort and unhappiness about the way things are going. In the Middle East, it could reflect a few moments of prayer.

## Comparing Values Across Cultures

| One Culture: | Another Culture: |
| --- | --- |
| Values change | Values tradition |
| Favors specific communication | Favors ambiguous communication |
| Values analytical, linear problem solving | Values intuitive, lateral problem solving |
| Places emphasis on individual performance | Places emphasis on group performance |
| Considers verbal communication most important | Considers context & nonverbal communication most important |
| Focuses on task and product | Focuses on relationship and process |
| Places emphasis on promoting differing views | Places emphasis on harmony and consensus |
| Emphasizes competition | Emphasizes collaboration |
| Prefers informal tone | Prefers formal tone |
| Is flexible about schedules | Emphasizes rigid adherence to schedule |

Gaining a thorough understanding of a people can take several years of living and working among them—and sometimes not even that is sufficient. However, you can increase your chances of achieving harmonious and profitable relationships by learning something about your associate's point of view and adjusting your behavior accordingly.

## Getting Along

Anyone who has traveled to another country has probably experienced an embarrassing moment or two caused by a cultural misconception or misunderstanding. To some extent, these are unavoidable and can be laughed off by both parties. In business, however, you want to do as much as possible to avoid such mishaps.

When cultures collide, as they inevitably will, the damage can be greatly reduced with knowledge, understanding and appreciation of what caused the collision.

## Passport Hong Kong

This book will introduce you to Hong Kong's business culture, offer some insights into the country and its people and help you understand how the local traditions, etiquette, values and communication styles differ from your own.

It is, however, only a beginning. Success will come from continuous learning through books and personal experience. This knowledge will make both your business and social transactions smoother and more enjoyable for everyone involved.

# Hong Kong Quick Look

| | |
|---|---|
| **Official name** | Hong Kong |
| **Land area** | 1060 sq km (409 sq mi) |
| **Largest city** | Kowloon, 2 million |
| **Elevations** | Highest—Victoria Peak, 398 m |
| | Lowest—sea level along coast |

**People**
- Population: 5,542,869 (July 1995 est.)
- Density: 5580 persons per sq km (14,400 per sq mi)
- Distribution (1994): 95% urban, 4% rural
- Annual growth (1995 est.) –0.12%

**Official languages**: Cantonese and English
**Major religions**: Buddhist, Taoist and Confucist 90%, Christian 10%

**Economy** (1994 est)
- GDP: US$136.1 billion / US$24,530 per capita
- Foreign trade: Imports—US$160 billion / Exports—US$168.7 billion
- Principal trade partners: China 33%, USA 22%, Japan 11%, Southeast Asia 7%
- Exchange (1996): HK$7.7337 = US$1

**Education and health**
- Literacy (1994 est): 77%
- Universities (1995 est): 7
- Life expectancy (1995): Women—83 years, Men—76 years
- Infant mortality (1995): 5.8 per 1,000 live births

# HONG KONG

## 2. Country Facts

### Geography and Demographics

Hong Kong is made up of parts of southeast China called Kowloon (literally "9 Dragons"), Tsuen Wan and Hong Kong Island, along with 235 other islands scattered across more than 2,900 sq km (1,130 sq miles) in the South China Sea. The metropolitan areas of Kowloon, Tsuen Wan and Hong Kong Island account for 15 percent of the land mass and are home to nearly all the population.

Before 1840, this hilly territory was sparsely populated with a few farms, fishing villages, and a pirate base or two. After China ceded Hong Kong to Britain in the Treaty of Chuenpi in 1841 (as spoils from the Opium Wars), traders began to settle on Hong Kong Island. (The Chinese saw this as a convenient way of ghettoizing the "foreign devils.") Soon, a flood of immigration from China began, peaking in the early 1980s.

The Hong Kong *yan* — Cantonese for *persons* — are 98 percent Chinese (*Han*) by language and ancestry. The other two percent are British, Indian, North American, Filipino, and other Asian and European citizens. Nearly 60 percent of the population is of Hong Kong birth, and the median age is just under 30. Every major religion is practiced, though ancestor worship predominates due to the strong Confucian influence.

## Climate

Although it lies 160 km (100 miles) south of the Tropic of Cancer, Hong Kong has distinct seasons. Beginning in September, a monsoon wind blows from the north and northeast, bringing cool, dry, sunny weather through December. The weather becomes more humid through winter, with temperatures falling lowest in February (13° to 17° C, 55° to 66° F). Around mid-March, a milder monsoon begins blowing from the south and southwest; gradually, humidity increases and temperatures rise until they reach 26° to 31° C (78°-87° F) in July.

Mid-summer brings typhoons, or what the Chinese call *tai-fung*, the Supreme Winds. Even with the warnings provided by modern technology, these storms can be terror incarnate. Born over the seas between Japan and the Philippines, typhoons can gust to over 210 km (130 miles) per hour. Hong Kong contains the only natural deep-water harbor — and therefore, the only shelter from typhoons — in that part of the world.

September and October are warm and sunny, making them the best months for travel.

## Business Hours

Most Western enterprises, as well as the larger Chinese business offices, banks and government departments, are open from 9 A.M. to 5:30 P.M. Monday through Friday, with a break for lunch from 1 P.M. to 2 P.M. Many offices keep late hours to accommodate international business. On Saturdays, hours are from 9 A.M. to 12:30 P.M. Retail stores are generally open every day of the year, except for the first two days of the Chinese New Year. In the prime shopping districts of Tsim Sha Tsui and Causeway Bay, shops usually open around 10 A.M. or 11 A.M. and stay open for twelve hours.

## National Holidays

New Year's Day .......... January 1
Chinese (Lunar) New Year*
................................... Late January, early February
                                 (lasts three days)
Ching Ming Festival* .. Early April
Easter......................... Friday and Saturday before and
                                 Monday after Easter Sunday
Tuen Ng (Dragon Boat or Double Fifth)
Festival....................... usually early June
Queen's Birthday ....... June 14 and following Monday
Liberation Day............ Last Monday and preceding
                                 Saturday in August
Mid-Autumn (Moon) Festival*
................................... Usually September
Chung Yeung Festival*
................................... Usually late October
Christmas & Boxing Day
................................... December 25 and first weekday
                                 thereafter

*Paid Legal Holiday

Other holidays of interest include the Lantern Festival (Yuen Siu) in mid-February; the Tin Hau Festival (May), which honors Hong Kong's goddess of fishermen and seafarers; and the Yue Lan Festival (September), when spirits of the dead receive food and burnt offerings (paper clothing, paper Mercedes Benzes, paper houses, paper money, paper stereos and VCRs, and so on).

# 3. The People of Hong Kong

## Language

Hong Kong has two official languages, Chinese and English, and they enjoy equal status in most communications between the government and the public. English is also widely understood and spoken in commercial and financial circles. The first bilingual legislation was enacted in 1989.

There may be as many as 1,000 different dialects in Chinese communication. Cantonese, the most widespread dialect of southern China, is spoken by almost all the Chinese population. (Hong Kong's vernacular Cantonese, colorful and always in flux, contains expressions like "swim-dry-water" to describe the breast-stroke motion used when shuffling mahjong tiles.) More and more people are learning to speak Putonghua ("common speech" or Mandarin), the official language of the People's Republic of China, partly because of increasing opportunities for travel and trade in the PRC and partly because, in 1997, the island will revert to Chinese rule.

Mastery of English is considered by many Hong Kong residents as a passport to a secure job. But during the last twenty years, the general level of English has declined — not due to official decree or even national sentiment, as in other parts of Asia, but to natural selection. Two decades ago, the young listened to American or British rock bands; today they have Cantopop. While "Anglo-Chinese" secondary schools are increasingly popular (231 out of 393 in the colony), a shortage of native English-speaking teachers has resulted in "Chinglish"-speaking students for whom English remains a foreign, rather than a second, language. And some of the more adept English speakers have emigrated to Australia, Canada and the U.S.

Learning a few Cantonese phrases will demonstrate your respect for your Chinese hosts. For the traveler limited to English only, the best approach is to speak slowly and simply; eliminate contractions and avoid colloquial expressions.

## Confucianism

Nearly all members of Hong Kong's financial and business community are familiar with most aspects of Western society; yet their character remains essentially Chinese. Furthermore, Hong Kong business is often linked to mainland China and other areas less intimate with Western culture. Consequently, foreign businesspeople operating in Hong Kong must grasp the values that shape the Chinese mentality, and these derive chiefly from the teachings of Confucius, who lived over 2,500 years ago. Confucianism is more of a guide for social behavior than a religion. Its tenets emphasize respect, duty, loyalty, sincerity and courage and were designed to contribute to the harmony of society — whether within the family, businesses, government or academia.

Confucius identified five kinds of relationships, each with clear duties:

**Ruler to People.** The ruler receives absolute loyalty from his people, who never question his motives or directives. In return, the ruler makes wise decisions and works only to better his people's lives.

**Husband to Wife.** The Confucian husband rules over his wife as a lord rules his people. She is obedient and faithful and provides her husband with sons. The husband is responsible for all his wife's physical needs.

**Parent to Child.** Children must show their parents love and respect and always remain unquestioningly loyal to their wishes, especially their father's. The parents are obligated to raise and educate their children; children must, in turn, care for their parents in old age.

**Older to Younger.** The Chinese have great respect for age, tending to link it with wisdom. Grandparents often rule a family; at the very least, they receive deferential treatment from children and grandchildren.

**Friend to Friend.** This is the only relationship between equals in Confucianism. Friends must be loyal and willing to help each other at every opportunity. Dishonesty between friends is a crime and demands punishment.

## How the Hong Kong Chinese View Themselves

While Westernization and competing philosophies have slightly diluted Confucist principles in modern Hong Kong, the latter continue to strongly influence Chinese behavior. Chinese tend to find that Western management styles emphasize product over people, whereas their business decisions tend to treat favored associates like members of what Westerners would call an extended family.

# The People of Hong Kong

The family is the preeminent institution in Hong Kong, and it serves as a great source of strength against life's vicissitudes. One's first duty is to the family's welfare, and working family members often pool their resources. Grown children often live with their parents, even if they are married (usually with the husband's parents).

Friends form strong bonds at every level of society. Same-gender schoolchildren can often be seen walking arm-in-arm, and longtime business associates call each other "Old Friends," a title indicating an especially close relationship. Chinese who respect each other will work hard to make each other successful. Favors and gifts between friends must constantly be reciprocated.

When a Hong Kong friend visits a friend, every detail of his or her stay may be prearranged; the guest may not be permitted to spend money on even the smallest items. However, when Hong Kong Chinese deal with strangers, they are often rude or uncaring. Such behavior is a psychological necessity in a city as densely populated as Hong Kong (or New Delhi, Paris or Tokyo). Crowds everywhere push and shove; no apologies are given and none are expected.

Humility remains an honored Confucian trait. Hong Kong Chinese rarely boast or outwardly show pride, even if their achievements are impressive. When Chinese are being polite, they can seem thoroughly self-deprecating.

## The Value of Face

Face (*mien-tzu*) is fundamental to the Chinese mentality. 'Having face' means having status among one's peers. Chinese are acutely sensitive to having and maintaining face in all aspects of social and business life. Face can be given, lost, taken away or earned. Causing someone to lose face can ruin your business prospects and even lead to retaliation.

Westerners can offend Chinese unintentionally by teasing them in the good-natured way common among Western colleagues. You can also take away someone's face by treating him less respectfully than his status requires.

Face can be given by praising someone in front of peers or superiors, or by thanking someone for doing a good job. Giving someone face earns respect and loyalty; look for opportunities to do so. However, avoid excessive praise; it will be interpreted as insincerity.

A person can lose face on her or his own by failing to live up to another's expectations, failing to keep promises, or by behaving dishonestly. Keep in mind that in business transactions, a person's face is not only his own, but also that of the entire organization he represents. Your relationship with the individual and the respect accorded him or her is probably the key to your business success in Hong Kong.

## Foreign Devils

The Cantonese word for foreigners is *quai loh* — foreign devils. All cultures believe, to some degree, that theirs is superior. An extreme, though uncommon, version of this attitude is for Hong Kong Chinese to regard all foreigners as hairy and apelike, smelling strangely and without any social graces: the lowest laborer is ten thousand times better than the best *quai loh*. A Westerner may be tempted, after many years of dealing in Hong Kong, to forget that she or he is a foreigner; the Chinese will never forget. Though these feelings are widespread, there are two advantages for the foreigner. First, the Chinese are proud of preventing private thoughts from interfering with public business. Second, the Hong Kong Chinese are an overwhelmingly practical people who understand the necessity of dealing with the West in order to both survive and prosper.

## Beliefs About Westerners

Some common Hong Kong perceptions of Westerners are:

- They are softened by growing up wealthy and lack the toughness that comes from waiting.
- Though often creative, they ignore the value of teamwork.
- They are motivated by selfishness and therefore lack patience.
- They make a show of friendship without sincerity.
- They are intolerant of other cultures.
- They are essentially a medium with which people in Hong Kong can make money.

Because personal relationships are so crucial in conducting business, the Hong Kong Chinese ambivalence about foreigners creates an informal but real barrier for outsiders wishing to enter this lucrative market. However, foreigners who commit to Hong Kong, who are willing to adapt to the culture, and who are very patient, will eventually succeed.

## How Others View the Hong Kong Chinese

The British founded Hong Kong as their emporium in the Far East. With few natural resources, Hong Kong's people had no choice but to turn to business and manufacturing for survival. Many locals and Chinese immigrants have made fortunes through shrewd investments and diverse partnerships.

Economically, the Chinese of Hong Kong are viewed as superlative middlemen, ferocious bargainers, unwavering friends — and unrelenting enemies. No one is better situated for, or more skilled in, dealing simultaneously with East and West.

## Sense of Identity

For much of its expatriate population, the newly arrived and the short-term visitor, Hong Kong must seem like an imperiled place. A superficial school of thought insists its current identity will vanish as of July 1, 1997 (when Hong Kong reverts to Chinese rule). But those born in Hong Kong or who have lived there for decades have an awareness of history that serves as irrefutable proof of survival. Created in the early years of Britain's empire-building, Hong Kong survived that nation's fall. Though captured by the Japanese in World War II, the colony celebrates its liberation annually. Hong Kong's economy boomed when mainland China became Communist and blossomed through the chaos of the Cultural Revolution. Deng Xiaoping's "Open Door" policies set Hong Kong firmly at the center of finance, shipping and marketing services for the entire region. Hong Kong has survived economic and physical disasters that have ruined other, seemingly invincible nations. By accepting the flow of change, Hong Kong *yan* have learned to find serenity in the timeless present.

# 4 Cultural Stereotypes

A visitor's perceptions of Hong Kong and its people may be based on personal experience, on what others have said or on stereotypes. These perceptions are almost certain to color both your social and business relationships. Those based on personal experience or valid research will probably be useful. Outdated or inaccurate information will create barriers.

While stereotypes about the people of Hong Kong vary, some are common.

## Superstitious

*Hong Kong Chinese are incurably superstitious and look for omens in everything.*

Open a door in Hong Kong and the past wafts in on you. When a culture has survived for millennia, some beliefs and customs become deeply imbedded. Throughout Hong Kong, you'll find signs, in both English and Chinese, forbidding spitting and announcing a fine. Yet the Chinese know an evil spirit-god lives in the throat; the spirit must be gotten rid of constantly or it will choke you. The law against spitting is therefore meaningless.

Many Chinese view the world as an essentially chaotic place, with events at the mercy of unpredictable gods. This seems depressingly fatalistic to Westerners. Yet the Chinese also believe that by observing natural patterns — in numbers, in weather, in the behavior of all living things — they can both avoid disaster and court success. All Western cultures have held similar beliefs and some continue to do so (former USA First Lady Nancy Reagan's dependence on her astrologer comes to mind). The Chinese honor such customs in the name of tradition.

## Superiority

*Other races are essentially beneath Chinese consideration.*

Hong Kong Chinese are inheritors of what is arguably the world's oldest continuous culture — and the first to produce printed books, silk, tea, gunpowder and much besides. "China" means "Middle Kingdom," the center of the world. The ancient Chinese were aware of other cultures but regarded them as no more important than ants running around the edge of a plate. Hong Kong Chinese are aware of this history. They understand that foreigners are human, that some are civilized, in their way, and that they are at the forefront of many technical fields. Yet at the core of even the most Westernized Chinese, a voice murmurs, "But we *are* better...."

## 1997

*Hong Kong is the only land that knows when it will die.*

Hong Kong was brought into existence as a British Crown Colony by several treaties forced on the fading Q'ing Dynasty (a result of the infamous Opium Wars). On December 19, 1984, the British and the People's Republic of China signed a Joint Declaration which states, in part, that on July 1, 1997, Hong Kong will become a Special Administrative Region within the PRC. The concept is called "One Country, Two Systems." Since the signing, tens of thousands have left the colony annually, shaken by the uncertainty of what this change may bring. Others express unbridled optimism while quietly obtaining foreign passports and establishing bases or bank accounts abroad. Still others have returned, anxious to take advantage of the transition. (The Chinese word for "chaos" combines ideographic characters meaning change and opportunity.) China has promised to preserve Hong Kong's way of life for fifty years, but as July 1997 gets closer, demands issuing from Beijing put that promise in question. Meanwhile, the government has embarked on large infrastructure projects to inject billions of dollars into the colony's economy by the end of this decade.

## Capitalism

*Hong Kong is full of predatory opportunists whose only concern is to make a quick profit.*

A Cantonese saying goes, *Moh ching, moh meng* — No money, no life. This is a reasonable approach to an environment rife with crowded conditions and seductive business opportunities. The tax rate is fixed in Hong Kong at about 15 percent; in practical terms, this means that a person who works an extra hour and makes an extra dollar gets to keep it. Nearly all Chinese work a six-day week and take only a few holidays each year. However, it is important to note that business relationships in Hong Kong are essentially personal, based on respect and trustworthiness. While the foreign entrepreneur with a guerilla approach to doing business may very well turn a quick profit, his long-term success in Hong Kong is unlikely.

## Provincial

*Hong Kong is a village masquerading as an international trade center.*

There is no masquerade. One the one hand, Hong Kong's economy is the eighth largest in the world; it is the premier bank and retailer of Asia. On the other hand, its expatriate population is as clannish as its Chinese. All news, gossip and speculation are published daily in Chinese newspapers, though only old China hands read them. For Westerners (the British in particular), the *Tattler* performs a similar service.

## Stiff Upper Lip

*The British in Hong Kong, like their counterparts in London, are impossibly stuffy and sexist.*

A large percentage of Westerners in Hong Kong are from the United Kingdom, and, like the rest of us, they drag their cultural baggage with them. The British do not lack strong feelings, but many have been raised in a tradition that eschews public displays of emotion — a tradition also prevalent, interestingly enough, in most Asian cultures.

As for regarding women as inferior: Although you may encounter some old-school die-hards, such unenlightened views toward "the fairer sex" have been all but eliminated during the past few decades. Most British men are willing to recognize a female colleague's merits and accept her on her own terms. The Chinese, as we will see in a few chapters, are another matter.

# 5. Regional Differences

## A Homogeneous People

Like most of the Earth's surface, Hong Kong has been taken over by a succession of increasingly aggressive tenants; the *quai loh* are only the latest in a series. Modern Hong Kong's people are descended from at least four ethnic Chinese groups: Punti, Hoklo, Tanka and Hakka.

The earliest written records date from before the eleventh century A.D., when the Han people (as the Chinese first called themselves) colonized China's southern coast. Early settlers on the hundreds of nearby islands called themselves Punti, meaning natives (an inaccurate term, since the Punti supplanted earlier aboriginals). The aboriginals may have formed the present Tanka, who were joined by the Hoklo, another fishing community from the coast of Fukien. Western visitors call the descendents of Tanka and Hoklo "boat dwellers." Today, over 200,000 spend much of their time afloat in Aberdeen or one of the other typhoon shelters around Hong Kong. Hoklo and Tanka derive most of their living by operating sampans that serve as harbor water taxis (popular with tourists), fishing, and other water-related commerce (i.e. smuggling).

The Hakka are the most recent arrivals, emigrating from the north in the 17th century. Hakka speak their own dialect and can be recognized in two ways: they wear straw hats with black cloth woven into the crown and around the brim; and the women work at construction sites, often carrying more than their body weight of stones or dirt in straw baskets suspended from a yoke over their shoulders.

The visitor will likely spend most of his or her time in the bustling metropolises on the Kowloon and Hong Kong sides — where few, if any, ponder the difference between the gentle pastoral and the bustling urban dwellers. Work and life are overlapping concepts in Hong Kong, united by struggle and enlivened by the joys all humans share.

# 6. Government & Business

Unlike nearly every other government in the world, Hong Kong's government has no formal development strategy. Its current "hands off" approach dates from the colony's beginnings: Rely on the marketplace to regulate itself and attract investment.

Foreign investment needs no official approval, though each company must register its interests with the appropriate government agencies. There are no specific structural requirements for foreign firms, other than that they comply with Hong Kong law, which is modeled on British common law. Virtually any contractual arrangement is acceptable and enforceable. The only capital requirements are for financial institutions needing licenses to operate.

## Barriers to Trade and Competition

Only two areas are not open to direct, unrestricted foreign ownership at present: the media and utilities. However, the government is currently considering plans to open up areas such as power and water utilities, communications and transportation, all currently dominated by firms operating under government monopoly franchises. It is even considering privatizing such government-controlled public works as highway and airport construction.

A free port, Hong Kong does not generally levy tariffs or duties on imports or exports, but it does set import quotas for certain items (like rice) and levy excise taxes on others. Import licenses are required for computers, peripherals, integrated circuits, disk drives, arms and ammunition, meat, radioactive substances, pharmaceuticals and pesticides.

To discourage automobile use in the crowded colony, Hong Kong slaps a hefty duty on imported vehicles. Car registration fees are based on the only logical standard for an environment severely threatened by pollution: the larger the engine, the higher the fee.

## 1997: Business As Usual?

The crucial question for Hong Kong's future is the Joint Declaration (see page 23), which leaves many specific issues about the British colony's upcoming "change of ownership" yet to be negotiated. Hoping to avoid the possibility of civic or student unrest, Mainland China amended the 1984 Declaration with the Basic Law (1990). Broadly stated, this document ensures that business will continue under essentially the same conditions after 1997 as are currently in force.

This jockeying for position between the mainland and its southern neighbor has encouraged the British to exercise their world-renowned diplomatic skills. It is not without irony that the English are attempting to chart a course to both placate the change-resistant Chinese old guard and retain as many of Hong Kong's trade concessions and social freedoms as possible. (In that spirit, the British have announced visa-free travel to the U.K. for Hong

Kong citizens after the colony's handover.)

A recent poll of top executives in ten Asian countries revealed that three out of five are pessimistic about Hong Kong's future as a financial center; only 15 percent believe its stature will grow after 1997. On the one hand, China will lose face if it does not seem firmly in control; on the other hand, it cannot afford to kill the goose that lays such golden eggs. (Almost 70 percent of all foreign investment in China flows through the colony. And the People's Liberation Army has substantial business interests in Hong Kong's bustling financial district.) While mainland Chinese speak of their sovereign rights over their capitalistic colony, the Hong Kong Chinese speak just as confidently about their pending economic freedom from British crown rule. In the meantime, emigration has slowed and business continues to boom.

## The Cachet of Old Friends

Some Western firms, most of them British, have been trading in Hong Kong for well over a century. Having proven their worth many times over, Chinese have granted these firms Old Friend status. Foreign companies new to Hong Kong may set their sights on this goal, understanding that it will, at the very least, require decades of unswerving effort. Of course, the Chinese conduct business with others besides Old Friends, but the terms are not as favorable. Even for insiders, the competition is unusually ferocious, and firms that "lose face" rarely get it back. These conditions are found in one form or another in most international markets; in Hong Kong, they are exponentially greater.

# 7

# The Work Environment

Although Hong Kong is relatively small and almost all its people are ethnic Chinese, generalizing about work styles and office environments is difficult. Management styles can range from traditional Confucian to the ultramodern lone Western entrepreneur, but they are usually a combination of the two. Everything depends on the executive's background and degree of Western influence.

At the risk of oversimplifying, business in Hong Kong is usually conducted formally, often following the British style. Punctuality is key; being late is seen as a lack of respect. Because Hong Kong is one of the world's most densely packed cities, working spaces are often cramped; a large office means high status. Allow yourself double the estimated time to arrive for meetings — the streets are always congested. Business proceeds at a rapid pace and appointments often change, so it pays to confirm them.

## Entrepreneurial = Buyer's Market

In contrast to Korea and Japan, companies in Hong Kong tend to be small and entrepreneurial.

Thousands of firms conduct the bulk of trade to and from China, and small back-alley garment shops employing ten people or fewer produce most of the colony's export textiles. This small scale of operation gives overseas businesspeople many opportunities; at the same time, it creates serious obstacles for larger companies wishing to lock out smaller competitors. This also complicates deciding which firms you should work with.

Prices are intensely competitive, and markups on production costs are minimal. These are two of the many reasons why Hong Kong is a shopper's paradise and a business purchaser's cornucopia.

## Hierarchy

Western democracies emphasize equality between individuals, while Confucius taught most humans are unequal. In ancient China, every person was born into a caste based on family background and occupation. The lowest classes were laborers; the highest, the Emperor and his family. Within each class was another system of rank, often with the youngest and least skilled persons in an occupation at the bottom and the oldest masters at the top. This arrangement heavily influences most Hong Kong firms.

The boss is often a ruler and father to his subordinates. Heads of large firms are called *tai-pans*, Cantonese for "supreme leaders." Workers have a duty to obey the boss and work diligently to help the company succeed. In return, the boss concerns himself with his workers' daily welfare and makes sure all their needs are met. Dealing with the company's enemies, as well as with any unexpected catastrophes, natural, human or demonic, are all his responsibility.

Age and rank are deeply respected. The young

are expected to obey their elders unquestioningly. Among coworkers, those with greater status and age command the respect of their juniors. Elders are expected to reward their juniors for work well done and to be sure their subordinates benefit from any success or honors the elders receive.

## Compradore = Go-Between

In the mid-nineteenth century, when Western firms (in Cantonese, *hongs*) began trading in Hong Kong, they hired Portuguese, along with Chinese and Eurasian businessmen, to act as intermediaries. (The Portuguese had been established in nearby Macau for centuries; "compradore" derives from the Portuguese word for "buyer.") The Chinese language, customs, and system of complex influences and obligations made it almost impossible for foreigners to transact business otherwise. Originally a house-steward, the compradore evolved into an official partner of and agent for China-based foreign establishments. All aspects of a business passed through their hands (and a little of everything stuck there).

Compradores are unique to Hong Kong companies. Chinese nationals often considered them to be little more than lackeys who cater to foreigners. As a matter of survival, these professional go-betweens had to possess a reasonable command of English and Western methods. These skills, combined with Chinese sophistication and enterprise, enabled some compradores to garner great power and influence. As a result, they contributed significantly to whatever economic progress China enjoyed in the nineteenth century. As with many traditional things in Hong Kong, this position continues to prove its usefulness in the modern world.

The nearest Western equivalent to the position

is that of a concierge in a first-rate hotel who expedites social and business interactions. During your earliest contacts with prospective Hong Kong associates, inquire about the identity of their compradore. His services will prove to be invaluable to your business ventures.

## Education versus Nepotism

Scholarship is a long-standing Chinese tradition, and formal education helps create influence and face. Hong Kong provides free compulsory schooling for nine years; entrance to the better secondary schools is based on competitive examination. Seven universities currently offer graduate degrees, but candidates far outnumber available openings. Many of the brighter, wealthier students take degrees abroad. Such degrees command special respect. Family connections can substitute, at least initially, for education, but no one tolerates a well-connected incompetent for long.

## The Hong Kong Work Ethic

To many foreigners, the long hours and sometimes frenzied pace of work in Hong Kong can seem less than humane, and the lives of low-income factory workers can be drab. But for the majority, hard work is an accepted way of life, and making money is viewed as an end in itself, not just a means to a better life. The Western concept of leisure is often interpreted as laziness.

## "Difficult" = No

Part of the definition of *tai-pan* is being the person who ultimately approves a deal; the foreigner should make whatever accommodations are necessary to identify and ultimately meet with the *tai-pan*.

Having done so, be aware that Hong Kong Chinese try to avoid saying "no" in order to avoid causing embarrassment or loss of face. They may say a particular item is "inconvenient" or "remains under consideration"; or they might say, "Yes, but it will be difficult." Bad news may be hinted at, or conveyed through an intermediary. Once a deal has been negotiated, some executives prefer to sign a short general agreement, leaving the details to be worked out later by others. Foreigners participating in joint ventures must accept this authority-at-the-top approach and abandon the consensus approach, since it will likely lead to misunderstandings and strained relationships.

## Feng Shui

No office building, store, residence or place of worship is built in Hong Kong without first consulting a *feng shui* man. His services are also required before a highway is laid, a telephone pole is erected or a tree is chopped down. According to tradition, every structure in China rests on some part of the Earth Dragon, over which flows Heaven-Earth-Air currents. A *feng shui* professional consults these currents to determine on which part of the Dragon a building rests. To rest on its back is ideal. Being on its neck or head is bad, and being on its eyeball means that a new site must be found.

Even in the best position, a building's interior must be aligned to prevent bad spirits from slipping in. The strategic positioning of a mirror can deflect or divert them; doors must never be in a straight line. Before the construction on Hong Kong's underground Mass Transit Railway began, a group of Taoist priests were hired to placate the spirits of the earth, whose domain was about to be violated.

Westerners are apt to find this custom quaint. But if you open an office anywhere in Hong Kong or mainland China, don't hesitate to consult a *feng shui* man. Your Chinese associates and local employees will see this effort as ensuring both their harmony and your business's prosperity.

# 8. Women in Business

## Traditional Roles

Many Chinese women view men as petulant children. But because husbands are the traditional breadwinners, wives and daughters are taught to exercise subtle control by creating a harmonious home, thereby helping to remove the poison men carry within them by nature. By being calm, tender, loving and understanding, Hong Kong women earn their advanced degrees in survival.

Women in the business arena are treated far better in Hong Kong than they are in many other parts of Asia, but Westerners rarely place them on an equal footing with men, and the Chinese, never. Considering women as equal business partners or as *tai-pans* is all but impossible for those bound by traditional thinking. Exceptions exist, but most executives are male with female secretaries.

## Changing Trends

Perhaps the strongest indicator of the changing role of women in Hong Kong is their image in the media, where they appear as busy and assertive, keeping their men waiting while they attend to their own priorities. In the past, women were designated as second signatories on their husband's credit cards. Today, the International Bank of Asia offers "My Card," a women-only credit card that allows applicants to qualify at a lower salary level than men.

Women who want a professional career tend to marry later and have fewer children; as of 1994, almost 28 percent never marry. Since Hong Kong Chinese tend to marry females with educations similar to their own, families tend to support daughters who pursue careers. If the daughter remains single, her income becomes part of the family resources.

Many travel agents, public relations executives and sales personnel are female. The traditional path of working up through a large company to highest possible position — personal assistant to the *tai-pan* — is fading. Some observers suggest that the influence of mainland China, with its greater gender equality, will bring further opportunities for women after 1997. (China's current Trade Minister, Wu Yi, is a woman.) In Hong Kong, women will most likely advance based on the same qualities that influence professional advancement for men: a keen sense of timing, the willingness to take risks, and the ability to win more than is lost.

## Strategies for Western Businesswomen

Women will find no shortage of sexism wherever they travel, and Hong Kong is no exception. Businesswomen must realize that they are dealing with a culture where maintaining or adding to their company's face is far more important than an individual's feelings. The business environment in Hong Kong is an inappropriate place to express political viewpoints or to point out that a culture's social behavior, established for millennia, is less than current.

Social change in Asia in general, and Hong Kong in particular, moves slowly and is unlikely to be significantly advanced by foreign presumption.

## Myth of the Blond Goddess

Outside of the cosmetics and fashion industries, it is unusual to find women heading trade delegations in Asia. For other fields, many companies consider balancing delegations with men if the leader is a woman.

Foreign businesswomen coming to Hong Kong should not encounter any overt discrimination. Sexual harassment is virtually unknown. However, it is important to maintain a serious manner and dress formally for every meeting. A woman's self-confidence and poise will be interpreted exactly as those qualities are in a man: signs of professional behavior that engender trust.

Chinese men sometimes hold tall, blond Western women in awe, partly because this is a rare combination in the Asian gene pool, and partly because heroines portrayed in Hong Kong cinema are often statuesque and fair-haired. Women should not regard this attitude as a disadvantage. Western influence is common enough that it may influence a Chinese to consider a woman who leads a team as exceptionally competent, since she holds such an important position.

# 9 Making Connections

## Potential Old Friends

As in mainland China and Taiwan, Hong Kong Chinese make little or no distinction between business and personal relationships. Newcomers should consider themselves as being constantly evaluated as potential Old Friends. Such a high level of respect and trust can take a decade or more to earn, but it means prosperity for your company measured in generations. Available capital, thorough research, cutting-edge technology and other resources mean nothing compared to personal commitment. Those who are successful belong to a loose network (of personal friends, friends of friends, former classmates, relatives and associates with shared interests) that can reach back for a century or more. Within such networks, people watch out for each other's interests and constantly seek to balance favors received with favors given.

The only area of business where personal connections are not crucial is export trade. Hong Kong has been exporting to the West for decades, but as selling overseas doesn't usually require close cooperation between the two sides, it is conducted relatively impersonally. (This does not apply to *joint*

Hong Kong export ventures Westerners may wish to establish.)

## Importance of Family

Throughout China, the family is seen as the only reliable fortress against a hostile world; it serves as a source of identity, protection, trust and strength. The reasons lie in history. China was often ruled more by decree than law. High officials could act with impunity, and innocent people lacking powerful friends to protect them often suffered great injustice. By establishing close connections with family members, other households and persons of high rank, the populace managed to survive, and sometimes even prosper, during centuries of adversity.

The social situation in modern Hong Kong is considerably less perilous than in ancient times, but the tradition of personal connections remains. Those within the clan work for its continued prosperity; those outside are regarded as inconsequential or potential threats.

## The Smell of Money

In this fast-paced, competitive atmosphere, where long-time residents claim to be able to smell the opportunity for making money, executives and entrepreneurs are constantly trying to maintain and extend their business networks. Though these networks (which extend to Guangdong Province in the People's Republic, Taiwan, Southeast Asia, Europe, and overseas to the Americas) exist for mutual profit, their criteria is the same as for personal networks: trustworthiness, loyalty and the repayment of favors. Cultivating friendships in Hong Kong is a fine art learned through practice and by paying attention to others' expectations and needs.

# 10 Strategies for Success

## Relationships Before Business

Western businesspeople prepare and present product campaigns, negotiate price and, if there's any time life over, consider developing a relationship with associates. Hong Kong Chinese consider this a backwards approach: how, they ask, can anyone enter into business without assessing a prospective associate's character and intentions?

Chinese formality is a screen that protects the face of both parties. Behind this impassive facade lies a deep concern for the quality of their personal relationships. Their concept of time takes the long view: Personal pleasure is too brief to be significant, whereas relationships can last for generations, and the time spent cultivating them is time well spent. Chinese are skilled in recognizing superficiality, haste, and lack of respect, and they avoid associating with those who display such traits.

## Ten Golden Rules

### 1. Establish Relationships

Establishing respect and trust is essential. Wait for the opportunities in each meeting to move beyond the preliminaries. Do not expect to come home from the first (or second or third) trip with a deal.

## 2. Find a Matchmaker

The best contacts in Hong Kong are made through a mutual friend. If this third party has close relationships with both sides, that alone may provide a basis for business. Finding a third party may be as simple as asking an overseas Chinese if she or he has any family members in Hong Kong with a business in your field. Anyone who has worked in Hong Kong, or who has dealt with persons there, is a potential contact source. Business consultants, both in Hong Kong and abroad, provide this advice for a fee. Chambers of commerce, small business associations, and Hong Kong government or international trade offices may also be of help.

## 3. Go to the Source

If you can't find a third party, consider making a fact-finding trip to Hong Kong. A Hong Kong trade show will allow you to display your goods or services while gauging your business prospects. Before leaving for Hong Kong, fax businesses with which you would like appointments. While some may not respond, others will have messages waiting at your hotel when you arrive.

## 4. Learn Patience

On your first few trips, concentrate on identifying possible candidates for future business relationships. Rushing into business before establishing a personal relationship will doom your enterprise. Evaluate each candidate carefully for strengths and weaknesses; you can be sure they are subjecting you to a similar process.

Once you have decided on prospective partners, plan on months of visits, gift giving, dinners and of offering small favors. Westerners may regard this as expensive and time-consuming; try to think of it as laying the foundation for long-term prosperity. Chinese appreciate all sincere efforts, and they never forget a favor. Be sure to keep an accurate account of the favors and gifts you receive; the odds are you'll be expected to reciprocate. Refuse these offers only if you have no intention of ever having a relationship; even then, make your refusal in the most polite terms in order to save face all around.

5. **Be Calm and Cordial**

Chinese prefer to conduct business in an atmosphere of harmony and cooperation. No matter what your inner frustrations or uncertainties, do not display them. Pretend to be unconcerned with deadlines or unexpected barriers — your self-control should become part of your negotiating style.

6. **Keep It Formal**

You may not be encouraged to treat your host informally for years; wait until the offer is extended. Chinese will be impressed with your discipline when you maintain an air of business formality. Clearly identify seniority and other roles as introductions are made. Your team should never disagree among themselves while in a meeting.

7. **Avoid Criticism or Complaint**

In a group setting, never refer to a failure on the part of a Chinese who is present or on the part of a colleague who is not; this causes irreparable loss of face and will destroy discussion. And never put a Chinese in a position where she or he must admit to failure. Either find a way to make an indirect reference to the problem (such as saying, "Perhaps next time, we could make another arrangement...") or ignore it.

8. **Be Modest**

Chinese appreciate the difficulty of creating flawless work and are delighted when the person responsible refuses to accept praise for it. This modesty indicates good character and upbringing. Cultivate this gracious attitude.

### 9. Leave Money Until Last

Price is often a primary Western consideration. Obviously, everyone's goal is to make money, but calling attention to that fact at a business meeting will only serve to label you as vulgar. Financial details should be the last matter discussed before signing a contract, and they are often settled by intermediaries.

### 10. Stay Detached

The actions of Chinese will at times appear to contradict their words (thus, their reputation for inscrutability). The art of negotiation is dealt with in depth in Chapter 13; for now, realize that you will often encounter what appear to be insurmountable barriers when conducting any kind of transaction in Asia. Without a sense of detachment, you will be easily overwhelmed. The more you can find ways to enjoy yourself, even if limited to private amusements, the better.

## Nicknames

Hong Kong businessmen who deal with Westerners sometimes adopt English nicknames (such as Charlie, Ed or Danny) and add these to their business cards. Consider reciprocating. If your name is Charles, for example, you might try using "Chas" (pronounced Choz, as in Oz).

On mainland China, there are no Eds or Dannys. But if you've been given a Chinese nickname, it's best to use it.

## The Expatriate's After-Hours Office

A great deal of expatriate business in Hong Kong is conducted outside the office. The visitor might be invited to accompany his or her Western host to a round of cocktail parties, held nearly every night except Sunday. These parties are not designed for relaxation. The idea is to show up and, glass in hand, find the person — perhaps more than one — you need to talk with. Agree to an interest rate, a sale of shares, the price of a container load; put down the drink, thank your host or hostess, and proceed to the next party. Westerners may make half a dozen whirlwind visits in a couple of hours and accomplish more than they did all day at the office. Should you embark on such a tour, remember to have only a sip or two of your drink at each stop. Hire a driver or have a cab waiting to help you complete your rounds expediently.

# 11. Time

Things move very quickly in Hong Kong. People are always arriving and leaving; most expatriates stay an average of two years. And there's always a crisis — business failure, corruption exposé, soaring or crashing stocks, a banquet or a typhoon. Even those not part of a major company are always on the move, planning, making money, or risking money to make more. Trips to the Philippines, Malaysia, Tokyo, New York, London, India and Beijing are commonplace; businesspeople are typically out-of-colony at least 15 working days a month. Months, even years, can whirl rapidly away.

## Deadlines, Chinese Style

Hong Kong Chinese understand the Western tendency to treat clocks and calendars like gods in constant need of propitiation. They will defer to this view for business purposes, but for the most part, their attitude is one of amused tolerance. Time is perceived as fluid. The Hong Kong Chinese do not compartmentalize their lives into seconds and minutes, weekends and holidays, and they resist saying "Monday" as though it were a place that could be pinpointed on a map.

Westerners pride themselves on being able to guarantee delivery dates; sometimes a product's quality suffers in the process. Chinese prefer to elicit consensus that an item is fully functional, wait until an auspicious moment, and then unveil a thoroughly tested prototype. Also, Chinese feel their culture has invented all the best ideas for government, art, philosophy and so forth. They are less interested in the bells and whistles of technological advance than in markets that will yield the highest profit and the best opportunities for expanding their ongoing networks.

This attitude influences the Chinese sense of time and of deadlines in at least two ways. First (at least until recently), delivery dates were viewed as rough guidelines. Dates incorporated into a contract are taken more seriously. Second, negotiations for joint ventures or distribution agreements may take an unusually long time (by Western standards) to negotiate, but once in place, the Chinese expect swift implementation.

## Appointments

The pace of modern business has made appointments more common than formerly, though Hong Kong Chinese still maintain a flexible attitude toward them. Appointments can be made by telephone at short notice, though if you inform business contacts of when you plan to be in Hong Kong, you'll likely find messages from them waiting at your hotel. Punctuality is important (both for business and social engagements), but allow the people you're meeting a thirty-minute leeway. This courtesy is designed to reflect their busy schedule and, more importantly, to add to their face.

Also allow extra time for traffic. There is only one rush hour in Hong Kong — it lasts from 6 A.M. to 9 P.M. Congestion and narrow streets make for plenty of accidents but few fatalities, since no one can go fast enough to cause serious damage. Most offices are easy to locate, but the tortuous streets of Kowloon require a map for the uninitiated.

You might consider taking advantage of Hong Kong's underground railway. It's as good as anything the West has to offer.

Hong Kong is currently in the midst of a US$20 billion construction frenzy. The just-completed Tsing Ma suspension bridge, the world's longest at 4,475 feet, connects Kowloon to Lantau — it's the first fixed crossing ever constructed between the island and the mainland. (It will be open to car and rail traffic in 1997.) Two other bridges, along with tunnels, highways, a new rail system and airport are also in the works.

# Business Meetings

## Preparation

Keep in mind that the Hong Kong Chinese tend to be more comfortable functioning as members of a group than as individuals. Generally, they assume that their approach is a universal one. Members of a visiting group who express opinions contrary to the groups's stated objectives will only cause confusion.

Every team needs a designated speaker who is also its senior member, with at least middle-level executive rank. The Chinese will look to that member for all major communication and accept his or her words as the voice of your organization. Your team leader should be patient, genial, persistent, have cross-cultural experience (especially in Asia) and the power to make binding decisions.

Before the meeting, supply your Hong Kong associates with a list of your team members and associates, ranked in order of seniority or importance. Hong Kong Chinese will evaluate the seriousness of a trade delegation by the rank of its members; if they know its head is a junior executive, the meeting will probably not succeed. They will probably wish to match your delegation with executives of similar status from their own firm. If the Hong Kong company sends someone to a meeting who is obviously low-ranking, this indicates that they have little interest in your proposals.

The visiting firm should also provide as much detail as possible about the issues under discussion. When dealing with a large Hong Kong company, schedule the meeting weeks in advance.

## First Day Protocol

Your team will be led into a room where your Hong Kong counterparts are already assembled. Your team leader should enter first. Teams sit across from each other at a table, leader facing leader, and the rest of the delegation seated in descending order of importance.

Don't expect to transact any business initially; your hosts will prefer to proceed slowly. This is a time for the senior members to get acquainted. Try to determine the Hong Kong members' status and their probable relations to each other. Since most companies are small, the head of the Hong Kong group may be the senior executive. Chinese management style emphasizes consensus. When your team has left, theirs may debate to determine a company position, but you will never witness such a discussion.

Chinese are gracious hosts; yours will probably have planned an itinerary that could take up most or all of the day. You may be treated to a factory tour, for example, followed by a traditional Chinese 10- or 12-course banquet.

## Small Talk First

Small talk always comes first. The Hong Kong leader won't move to business matters until he

# Business Meetings

thinks everyone is comfortable. He will deliver a short welcome speech, then turn the floor over to the visitors. Your senior team member should speak for your company, addressing only the senior Hong Kong man. Chinese prefer to hear a proposal as a broad overview, rather than as a point-by-point dissection of specific issues. The details will come later.

Without boasting, your senior member should emphasize all the positive outcomes of the future relationship, stressing mutual benefits. Use broad strokes and speak in a leisurely manner, avoiding any appearance of pressure. Visual aids and written materials are often useful. Mention any awards or complimentary reviews of your past work; Chinese want to be associated with winners.

Tea may be served. Don't touch yours until the host begins. If he lets the tea sit untouched for a long period, this may be a signal that he considers the meeting over and is waiting for you to thank him and rise.

## Concluding the Meeting

Look for a signal from the Hong Kong team leader — he may simply allow silence to continue for some time before he stands. Once he thanks everyone, your group should leave. As a matter of face, avoid any discussion until your group reassembles at a new location, preferably somewhere private, like your hotel room.

# Negotiating with Hong Kong Chinese

The first-day protocol of greetings, small talk, touring and banqueting may encourage foreigners to assume that their subsequent business dealings will proceed as smoothly. This is possible but unlikely. Lavish, pre-negotiation entertainment is partly an attempt to soften the delegation and thus gain a bargaining advantage. Hong Kong Chinese are tough negotiators and will subject every aspect of a potential deal to rigorous inquiry. Westerners should be prepared to encounter fury, flattery and every possible emotion in between.

## Global View

After the visitor outlines his team's position (see previous chapter), the Hong Kong team leader takes the floor and answers point by point, remedying any perceived omissions. From this point, negotiations will take on the rhythm of a formal debate. The Hong Kong approach is to begin with a global view of the entire proposal, then break it down into major sections in which concrete issues and problems can be addressed.

## A Penchant for Detail

Be prepared to provide lengthy explanations, reviews and summaries. The Hong Kong team will request recesses and delays of unstated lengths while they adjourn to consult, or to reconsider its position on a point. Westerners may be worn down by this seemingly endless circling and repetition, and that is partly its purpose. But it's also true that Chinese love to scrutinize each detail and consider all possible consequences.

The long hours of negotiation serve three important functions. First, they help form the basis of a relationship that, if lasting, will prove much more important than any one written contract. Second, this time permits both sides to work on resolving the many potential misunderstandings inherent in cross-cultural communication. Third, discussing issues (which may at first appear peripheral) will help prevent implementation problems later on.

## The Serenity of Chess

Use the above-mentioned breaks in discussion to think of positive ways to present an issue. Avoid being confrontational. Reject nothing, even if you are privately opposed. Westerners are used to dealing directly and swiftly; this style must be avoided in Hong Kong. Think of the outwardly casual pace of a chess game; in reality, the opponents are furiously engaging in war without blood.

A good way to promote harmony is to practice excellent manners, which, for Westerners, means focusing on restraint. Avoid familiarity and use last names with an appropriate title. Always observe rank in seating arrangements and introductions. Do not interrupt, raise your voice, or openly disagree with your teammates. Never show impatience through your facial expressions or by fidgeting. If you say something that gives offense, don't hesitate to apologize. Play the game by Hong Kong rules. Your potential partners want both sides to win, with perhaps a small advantage for themselves.

## Shrewd Tactics

Hong Kong negotiators are very good at protecting the interests of their clients. Some of their more common tactics are:

- **Controlling the schedule and location.** The Chinese are aware that most foreigners have spent considerable time and money to reach Hong Kong and that they don't want to leave empty-handed. The Hong Kong team may appear indifferent about whether or not negotiations produce a deal, and then, late in the game, make what the visiting team considers excessive demands.

- **Threatening to take their business elsewhere.** Sometimes the Chinese will negotiate with several competing companies at once. They may let this be known as a way of applying pressure to secure a better deal.

- **Using friendship to gain concessions.** Chinese who have established relations with Westerners may remind them that true friends work for maximum mutual benefit. Look at your agreement carefully to see that the benefits are evenly shared.

- **Showing anger.** Although Confucian morality forbids displaying anger, Chinese may pretend to be upset in order to increase the pressure. If your team shows fear about losing the contract, this ploy has succeeded.

- **Sensing the other side's tension.** If the Chinese

know that your job depends on getting a contract, they will probably demand additional concessions.

- **Flattery.** Chinese are not above heaping praise on foreigners either for personal attributes or business acumen. Don't let their skill in ego-building give them an advantage. They, themselves, are uneasy about accepting compliments; theirs may not always be as sincere as one might presume.
- **Knowing when you have to leave.** The Hong Kong Chinese may delay substantive negotiations until the day before you plan to depart in order to pressure you into a hasty agreement. Counter by making departure reservations for several dates, and be willing to stay longer in order to ensure success.
- **Attrition.** Hong Kong negotiators are patient. After all, you came to them, and they're looking for ways to wear you down. This is not a lack of caring but a method of assessing your character. Excessive evening entertainment, especially when coupled with jet lag, can take the edge off your attentiveness.
- **Examining your words for inconsistencies.** Chinese subordinates take careful notes at discussions, and they may quote your own words back at you to refute your position. Your best approach is to do the same.
- **Inflating prices and hiding their actual cost.** Hong Kong negotiators may appear to agree with your demand for lower prices, but their original estimates may have been artificially high.

## Tips for Foreign Negotiators

Various tactics may help in dealing with Hong Kong Chinese.

- **Be totally prepared.** The most effective negotiator knows every aspect of the business deal. At least one member of your team should be technically oriented and, when instructed, be able to display that knowledge in negotiations. The Chinese will have at least one person who can match that knowledge. Be ready to give a lengthy, detailed presentation of your side of the deal.

- **Play off competitors.** When you encounter obstacles, consider letting the Chinese know they are not your only option. Cutthroat competition is the norm in Hong Kong, and you can probably find a matching offer elsewhere. If price is the problem, consider looking at mainland China or elsewhere in Southeast Asia. If quality is your concern, Japanese companies may be able to outperform Hong Kong producers.

- **Be willing to leave.** Let the Chinese know that failure to agree is preferable to a bad deal.

- **Cover every detail before signing a contract.** Be certain that both parties understand their obligations. Assumptions often increase the distance between cultures and can put you at a serious disadvantage.

- **Take detailed notes.** Review what the Hong Kong side has said, and clarify any ambiguities.

- **Inflate your price, at least initially.** If you're selling, start high (it's expected) and negotiate from there. If buying, do the opposite.

- **Ignore contradictory behavior.** Your genial host from the previous night may become impersonal and detached when sitting across

the bargaining table. When you match this behavior, the Chinese know your first priority is doing good business.
- **Be patient.** Chinese assume all Westerners are in a hurry. They may try to encourage your agreement before you have had a chance to examine the details thoroughly.
- **Profess fairness.** Tell the Hong Kong leader your relationship will grow stronger only with a mutually beneficial arrangement.
- **Be willing to compromise without conceding too much.** The concept of face can be used to your own advantage by letting your counterparts know how unrealistic concessions might negatively impact your company.
- **Adopt the Chinese view.** Most Westerners approach business (and much of their lives) as something to get through — this week, this month, this season. The Chinese businessperson plans for decades, knowing that with foresight and good luck, he can become an ancestor. (There is little distinction between an ancestor in lineage and one who initiates an ongoing business connection.) Allowing some leeway over a specific issue may garner greater overall benefits in the future. The trick is to be flexible without seeming weak. Insist that each concession you make must be matched.

## The Language Barrier

Most Hong Kong Chinese involved in international business are used to negotiating in English, but it is still a second language for them. Any businessperson spending more than a few weeks in Hong Kong each year will find a basic knowledge of Cantonese useful. When negotiating in English, speak slowly, don't use slang or jargon, and don't move to a new point until you are certain your current point is thoroughly understood. Realize that anything you say will almost certainly be taken literally.

Having an interpreter of your own can be expensive but helpful, especially in sensitive negotiations. Your interpreter should be multicultural as well as multilingual, sensitive to feelings and intonations in both languages. A qualified interpreter can help clarify points, provide counsel on the best way to present issues and advise you on the reactions of the other side. Make sure your interpreter has adequate command of the technical language your discussions may involve.

Ideally, you should locate an interpreter in advance. But even after you've arrived in Hong Kong, your hotel can refer you to organizations that provide interpreters and translators.

## Tips on Using Interpreters

### 1. Establish Guidelines

Before a meeting, discuss the mechanics of how you will work together. Provide your interpreter with as much written material as possible. Give him or her time to become familiar with your style, humor and body language. This will help ensure that your messages are conveyed accurately.

### 2. Don't Exhaust Your Interpreter

During a meeting or negotiating session, stop every few sentences to allow for interpretation, and try to limit each sentence to one main point. Interpreters should rest at least every two hours. If negotiations are to continue for more than a day, you may need two interpreters. Using an interpreter can stretch a meeting to three times its normal length, so be patient with the flow of discussion.

### 3. Review What's Been Said — Anticipate What's Coming

After a meeting or during breaks, review with your interpreter the main points made by both sides. Ask what your interpreter observed about the other side's position or behavior. Work together to get a feel for the direction in which negotiations are headed, and anticipate what will need to be said later on. Doing this helps your interpreter to prepare the interpretation so that your views will be received in the most favorable possible way.

### 4. Emphasize Important Points As They Arise

Abstract and complicated discussion is seldom directly translatable; an experienced and qualified interpreter tailors translations in each language to reflect their style, level of formality, tone and intended meaning.

## Contracts, Hong Kong Style

A few years ago, many Hong Kong Chinese viewed written contracts as virtually meaningless. What mattered were personal commitments between associates. This view still predominates in mainland China, but under Hong Kong law, a contract is a legally binding document.

Westerners prefer the letter to the spirit of a contract. Some Hong Kong Chinese see a contract as a loose commitment, rather than a document outlining all details of a business relationship; some Asian executives would rather sign a short agreement of principle, allowing subordinates to work out the details later. This situation can create costly delays and misunderstandings.

During negotiations, always remember Hong Kong Chinese tend to view any deal with foreigners as one component of a larger, ongoing relationship. The immediate issues are seen as building blocks designed to strengthen reliability and cooperation. Those who wish to conduct long-term business in Hong Kong need to accept and implement this very practical (if non-Western) approach.

# 14. Business Outside the Law

## Underground Economy

Underground economies are traditionally begun and maintained by outsiders; Hong Kong is too ethnically homogeneous for such an arrangement. However, there is a long-standing network that operates independently of legal restraints — providing everything from powdered rhinoceros horn (an alleged aphrodisiac) and antique porcelain to "designer" drugs and the hottest new Western children's toy.

## The Triads

Shortly after Hong Kong became a British colony, government officials discovered the presence on the island of what they first called anarchists. These men were known by many names: Red Party, Red Brotherhood, Heaven and Earth Society. Hung Mun or Hung Tong — *tong* meaning "secret brotherhood" — were the most common Cantonese names. Already well established in southern China, Tong members earned their living chiefly by extorting protection money, or *h'eung yau* (fragrant grease), from every prostitute, merchant, gambling establishment and restaurant, peasant and landowner. Those who refused were mutilated or killed. Every Tong member paid dues to the organization, like in an outlaw trade union.

Since this organization used a red triangular flag as a symbol, Westerners began calling them Triangs, or Triads. Though the Triads never realized their long-term goal of overthrowing the Q'ing Dynasty and restoring its predecessor, the Mings, to power, they managed to establish an unshakable hold in Hong Kong, Macau, Shanghai, Singapore, and other Chinese population centers (including San Francisco's Chinatown, which was torn by Tong Wars from 1880 until the Big Quake of 1906).

Today, the Triads are likely to be involved in any nefarious activity, with drug trafficking as a primary source of wealth. Consider the following paradox: drug use in Hong Kong has not noticeably declined, yet since 1987 the number of serious offences reported and of persons prosecuted has steadily dropped, with seizures of narcotics plummeting. These facts suggest one of two things — either a higher quality of law enforcement than any other place on the planet, or that the Triads continue to exert their time-honored influence. The world center for the growing, processing and sale of narcotics (opium and cocaine, in particular) is the Golden Triangle, whose points lie in Vietnam, Laos, and the Yunnan Province of China. It's noteworthy that the latter is located within convenient transportation distance of Hong Kong.

## Graft and Corruption

Cash, unofficially and judiciously applied, is a feature of most major governments. Hong Kong's corruption, compared with that of Taiwan or Korea, is kept within decent bounds. This is partly because

# Business Outside the Law

Hong Kong remains untroubled with democracy and politics, and partly because there are always opportunities to make money illegally.

It's also worth noting that the liberal use of cash is often seen as an extension of the practice of gift-giving (see Chapter 17), rather than as outright corruption.

The police have supplied the most frequent examples of corruption, such as in the 1990 trial of a senior narcotics officer in the Customs and Excise Department charged with smuggling fifty kilos of heroin into Australia. But reformers who expose such behavior rarely find their efforts, in the end, to have been worthwhile. Criminal paybacks often take the form of honors awarded or offices allocated, rather than cash dispensed, making such activities difficult to prove and almost impossible to curtail.

## "The Emperor is far away...."

The Independent Commission Against Corruption, established in 1975, claims to have overcome large-scale crime while admitting that small-scale graft continues. The current governor, Chris Patten, rules for the Crown through a legislative council. Both ICAC and Patten listen to the business community, but social change occurs very slowly.

China has taken the position that the future governor or mayor of Hong Kong must be a Chinese citizen. There is no reason to indicate that any of these factors will significantly alter the workings of Hong Kong's shadow economy. A Cantonese saying runs, "The mountains are high, and the Emperor is far away," suggesting that people will always find a way to avoid the constraints of laws and rulers.

## Names & Greetings

### A Multiplicity of Names

When asked their names, Chinese people will more often than not give their surname (family name) first, followed by their given name. The surname is usually monosyllabic, with the given name having two syllables (though single-syllable given names are not uncommon). For example, Deng Xiaoping's surname is Deng and his given name is Xiaoping. Lu Xun, a famous author of the early twentieth century, has a single-syllable given name: Xun. Each syllable is the pronunciation of a single written character.

To add to this complexity, all Chinese have four names: one at birth, another during puberty, a third at adulthood and one each person uses privately. As for surnames, Chinese call themselves *lao-tsi-sing* — the Ancient One Hundred Names. There are actually a few thousand surnames, which is still a small sample to distribute among over a billion persons. Several different persons might share the surname Yu, but each may pronounce it differently, and it is entirely possible that none will be related.

## Gender and Designations

Addressing the Chinese by their first or given name(s) is not appropriate, even if they have told you what they are; first names are reserved for family and close friends. Decades of Western influence have encouraged Hong Kong Chinese to adopt English names and/or to invert their names so that the surname follows the given name, such as Sally Lau. In such cases, it's usually fine to call her Sally. If you're not sure if a name *has* been inverted, assume it hasn't.

Typically, men address each other by their surnames. Good friends, particularly those under the age of thirty, add a long *a* to each other's surnames (*a Lau*). Older males are sometimes addressed by adding the respectful prefix *lo* (*lo Lau*). Such courtesies are usually not extended to foreigners.

Generally, wives don't adopt their husband's names when they marry. However, it's acceptable to call a married woman either Madame (followed by her maiden name) or by her husband's surname (Mrs. Chan).

People outside the family almost never use each other's first names, even if they are very close. Westerners should use Mister, Miss or Mrs. when addressing Chinese, just as they do in Western society.

## The Beauty of Cantonese

In English, we say a person's title first (Doctor, Professor), followed by the first, middle and last names. In Cantonese, the surname is addressed first, followed by given and second names, with the title last. Doctor Qi Qing Xu becomes *xu qi qing bok si*. The beauty of Cantonese is that, if you can't remember or you don't know someone's surname, addressing them by their title alone — Doctor,

Teacher, etc. —is fairly acceptable. A teacher with the surname Yuan can be referred to as Teacher Yuan. This form of address applies to company managers, directors and higher-ranking officials.

## Terms of Respect

Younger people always treat their elders with deference, as the following terms indicate. A younger person meeting an older woman for the first time may call her auntie (*a yi*); a man can be called uncle (*suk suk*). *Baak baak* is used to address a female or male roughly one's parent's age. Granny (*poh poh*) is an appropriate term for an elderly female and *sai baak* for an elderly male.

As a foreigner, your best approach is to ask people how they wish to be called.

## Shaking Hands

Traditional etiquette calls for saluting another by making a fist with the left hand, covering it with the right palm, and shaking the hands up and down. Some Chinese still do this, especially with close friends. It is also a formal way of saying thank you and is used as a sign of reverence.

When meeting Hong Kong businesspeople, display sincerity and respect. Handshaking has successfully been imported from the West, though it varies in some ways. Chinese tend to shake hands very lightly, without the Western motion that suggests working a pump handle. Chinese may stand closer to you than people do in the U.S. or Europe, and a handshake may last as long as ten seconds.

## The Importance of Business Cards

The handshake is always followed by an exchange of business cards; bring plenty, preferably with English text on one side and Chinese characters on the other. It's worthwhile to seek out expert advice on which characters to use, since some ideograms have more favorable connotations than others.

Give and receive cards with both hands, holding each card corner between thumb and forefinger. When accepting a card, take a few moments to study the text. Showing respect for the card's message demonstrates respect for the person it represents.

## Protocol

When the Chinese greet someone, they lower their eyes as a sign of deference. A visitor should refrain from looking intensely into a host's eyes.

Presenting letters of introduction from well-known business leaders, overseas Chinese, or former government officials who have dealt with Hong Kong is an excellent way to show your status and emphasize the seriousness of your intentions. Chinese are deeply concerned with social standing, and anything you can do to enhance their regard for you will be rewarded. Be careful not to appear arrogant. Confucian morality condemns such behavior.

# 16. Communication Styles

## Consider the Context

The Hong Kong Chinese tend to be reserved and conservative, especially when meeting new people. This reserve doubles when meeting foreigners. Their communication style is often implicit and nonverbal; in a word, contextual. Below are some common traits of Hong Kong Chinese communication.

- People you have recently met will ask your age, the amount of money you make, your marital status and other personal questions. This is intended to show concern; reply frankly.

- Especially in the early stages, business conversations include questions, and often lengthy discussions, about both parties' family and friends.

- Remarks about politics, religion or divorce may be considered offensive or insulting.

- Westerners joke to relieve tension. This is acceptable behavior during informal situations but not during a business presentation or speech. Sexual jokes are acceptable only in private between intimate partners. Cross-cultural humor is rare and usually not understood; best avoid it.

- The Chinese often tell a person what they believe she or he wishes to hear, whether or not it is true. This is considered courteous, although it can lead to problems for Westerners. The best way to avoid frustration with this subtlety is to explain to your Chinese co-workers that you appreciate direct communication and that bad news will not upset you.

## Nonverbal Communication

Though the Chinese have been in contact with Western culture since the Ming Dynasty, the Western tendency toward public displays of affection (kissing someone hello or good-bye, throwing your arms around someone's shoulders) bothers them. Still, the younger Chinese generation is likely to be seen holding hands or walking arm-in-arm with friends. As a foreigner, the safest and most face-saving nonverbal tactic to employ is smiling.

Winking, eating food in the street, blowing your nose in public and chewing gum are all considered impolite. Pointing with the forefinger is seen as an accusatory gesture. To indicate someone or something, use the entire hand, with the palm open.

## Guidelines

The following will help you become conscious of your body language and the ways in which it might be interpreted.

### 1. Avoid Physical Contact

Lightly touching another person's arm when speaking is a sign of close familiarity. Except for shaking hands, do not offer to touch anyone unless you know them very well. Women should be careful not to brush against a monk or Buddhist priest (they are forbidden to touch women).

## 2. Keep Your Distance

Westerners typically stand less than a meter apart in formal situations. Hong Kong Chinese are more comfortable at a distance of a meter or slightly more. Standing closer than that will probably force your conversation partner to retreat until they are backed up against a wall.

Informally (in a karaoke bar, for example), Chinese will permit the earlier barrier to shrink by nearly half. Westerners may be surprised by the sudden change and be tempted to interpret it as a sign of increasing intimacy. But the next morning, the usual distance will have been reestablished.

All proximity barriers are suspended when walking on the street, in lifts (British for elevators), on public transportation, or in any unavoidably crowded place. Don't expect an apology when you're jostled; it's part of the Hong Kong experience.

## 3. Speak Softly

Most Westerners find a low, soft voice with careful diction is persuasive. In Hong Kong, keep the low tones but slow down slightly. At least some of your audience will not have English as their first language. A loud voice or raucous laughter will identify you as rude and uncontrolled.

## 4. Keep Your Hands Down

Cantonese, the dialect you will hear most often, can have as many as ten tones for the native speaker (though Westerners rarely manage to hear more than six). With such subtlety in pronunciation, Hong Kong Chinese rarely resort to physical gestures while speaking. Therefore, they regard large-scale hand and arm movements as unrefined (at the very least) and possibly even threatening. Small, discreet gestures to illustrate a point are much appreciated.

5. **Listen More, Talk Less**

The Chinese value tranquility in all things, even business meetings; be prepared for a slower pace than you're used to. Let your hosts speak first, and wait until they are done talking before you reply. Plan what you will say, so that your remarks are cogent and concise. Sharp listening skills are useful in Asia.

6. **Posture Counts**

T'ai chi, the most common exercise in Hong Kong (see Chapter 17), stresses physical equilibrium, as do many elements of Chinese culture. An erect, relaxed stance is interpreted as a sign of alertness and control. Slouching, leaning back in a chair or leaning against a doorframe will only serve to alienate you. Pointing your foot at someone, exposing the sole of your shoe by crossing your legs, or (heaven forbid) putting your feet up on a table or desk is considered particularly impolite.

Chinese usually stand with their hands at their sides. When sitting, they keep their legs together and place their hands in their laps or on top of the table. The Western male habit of standing with hands in pockets is considered distasteful.

7. **Remember Your Status**

Do what you can to emphasize your host's importance, especially if you are physically larger. When passing in front of a seated Chinese, hunch over slightly to acknowledge his presence. Never forget that you are a guest. Your manners (more than any business offer you may make) will determine whether you will be invited to return.

# 17  Customs

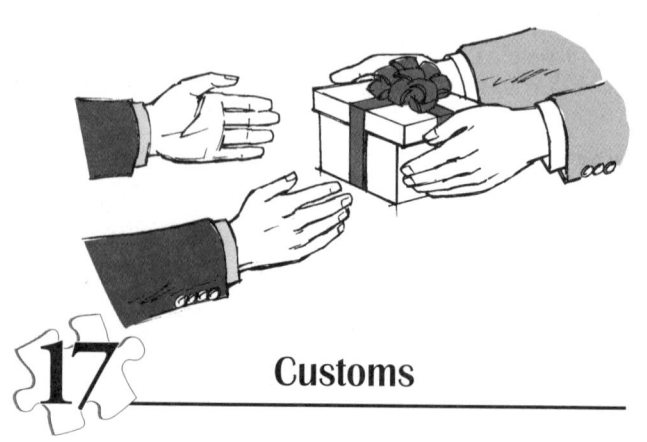

### Gift Giving

Chinese give gifts to express friendship, to symbolize hope for good future business, to conclude a successful enterprise, to show appreciation for a favor, or to celebrate Chinese New Year. Foreign businesspeople should take time to choose appropriate presents for their hosts. The Western habit of a simple verbal "Thank you" is considered glib and superficial. A gift is tangible evidence of sincerity. Its symbolic value exceeds its cost; therefore, avoid expensive gifts unless the recipient is an Old Friend.

Business-related gifts, such as pens or paperweights with your company logo, are appropriate if your first visit is to a host's office. If you choose only one gift, give it to the head of the group at dinner or at the successful conclusion of a meeting. Giving a pair (2) of anything is considered auspicious. When giving gifts to members of a group, be sure that they are all of approximately equal value, or that the chief executive's gift has the greatest value. Leave no one out.

When visiting someone's home, fruit, candy or a memento of your country (a photo calendar or

# Customs

gourmet food item, for example) will be welcome. Avoid flowers (they're usually associated with funerals), clocks (they symbolize death) and scissors or other sharp objects (they suggest a relationship is over). Perfume for a host's wife or toys for children indicate your concern for the entire family. Foreign liquor, especially French cognac, is appreciated when your relationship is well-established. When giving gifts, make sure the wrapping paper is red or gold. Blue, black and white are mourning colors.

As in the case of business cards, the polite way to present and receive gifts is with both hands outstretched. Using only one hand is considered rude.

Don't be surprised if the recipient refuses the gift two or three times; quick acceptance is equated with greediness. Watch carefully: if your Chinese host appears embarrassed when refusing, insist that the gift is only a token of your respect and that you would be honored if it were accepted. Usually, after some delay, Hong Kong Chinese will graciously accept. If, however, the gift is rejected several times in a serious manner, withdraw the offer. The recipient may not wish to begin a relationship with you and does not want to be in your debt.

## Gift Receiving

When a gift is offered to you, the refusal ritual is not necessary. Accept humbly, with a few words of thanks. The gift may be simply a courtesy, but it could also signal that your host wants a relationship or that you will be asked for a favor. Remember to reciprocate, whether asked or not.

If the gift is wrapped, don't open it in front of the giver unless he or she urges you to do so. If that's the case, take your time; hastily tearing it open will be seen as childish, greedy behavior.

## Taking the Waters

Primarily an import from Shanghai, Hong Kong's public baths can be a pleasant way to pass a few hours. Their purpose is essentially recreational, so if an associate brings you as a guest, don't expect to discuss business there.

You'll start by checking in at a desk. For the modest fee, you will receive a key with an elastic cord; slip the cord over one wrist. The baths are separated by gender. Go upstairs or to another section of the ground floor, where you will find a cubicle whose number matches your key. Inside are two single beds, each with at least two towels neatly folded on top, some paper or plastic slippers, a small drawer unit between the beds, and hangers for your clothes. Place your valuables in the drawers, which the key locks.

Drape one towel around your waist and the other over your shoulders; put on the slippers. Leave the cubicle section and find the sauna. Hang your towels on a hook outside, take off the slippers and enter. You may stay as long as you like. Then put the towels and slippers back on and shuffle to a nearby row of sinks. Fill one with whatever temperature of water you prefer and refresh yourself with the washcloth provided.

Next, proceed to the bathing room. It contains what looks like a shallow swimming pool with broad tile edges. Doff the slippers and towels and lie down on the tile. An attendant will provide a small wooden support for your neck, soap the front of your body, rinse you off, then motion for you to turn over and repeat the process. Then you may enter the pool, where you may swim slowly or soak for a minute or two.

Dry off, don the towels and slippers, and return to your room; a pot of tea will be waiting on top of the drawer unit. Also waiting will be another attendant, who will provide a massage, followed by a gentle walk along the length of your spine. Afterward, sip the tea at your leisure, dress, and leave the key in the drawer's lock.

## Tai Chi Ch'uan

Many Westerners profess a dedication to vigorous physical exertion which, they feel, maintains their image as avidly competitive and impressively disciplined. If that's your style, check to see whether or not your hotel has exercise facilities or ask your Hong Kong host if his company has a membership in a local sports clubs.

Hong Kong is home to several golf courses, as well as squash and tennis courts (both public and private). Windsurfing centers rent equipment and offer lessons. Repulse Bay is a popular swimming beach.

Or you might consider a time-honored Eastern alternative. Early in the day, and in all weathers except typhoon or heavy rain, Chinese of all ages congregate in the city's parks and plazas to perform *t'ai chi ch'uan*. *Tai chi* dates back to the 14th century, when a Taoist monk witnessed a fight between a white crane and a snake; he devised a system of 36 defensive postures based on the movements of birds, horses, monkeys and clouds. The various forms of this martial art were guarded secrets until this century. Though *tai chi* may look easy, even top athletes will find it challenging. Dress in loose clothing, stand at the back of a group, and follow their motions. A full cycle will take approximately 20 minutes, but you can stop at any point.

# 18. Dress & Appearance

Hong Kong has long been recognized as a garment assembly center, thanks in part to the many tailors who fled here from Shanghai shortly before it fell to the Japanese in World War II. Imported and locally made fashions for both men and women can be found in abundance, and at realistic prices. Custom-made clothing is popular and relatively cheap. Count on at least two fittings.

You will encounter all styles of clothing in Hong Kong. The traditional *cheong-sam* (a formfitting sheath with side slits, high collar and frog closures, sometimes made of brocade) can still be found, though it's not as common as it was thirty years ago. Hong Kong women favor top designer fashions, jewelry, cosmetics, shoes, handbags and watches. Good-quality blue jeans are acceptable in public. The young favor the latest American and European fads.

The business community dresses conservatively, in the style of major Western business venues. Suits and ties are the uniform for men, skirts and blouses, dresses or suits— but not pantsuits — for women.

The quality and design of your clothing will be

# Dress & Appearance

noted by your Asian counterparts and, generally speaking, you will be judged by them far more than you would be in the West. Dark or muted colors are most common. Carrying a well-made attaché case is considered stylish and prestigious for both genders.

Summers are hot and humid. Sandals are considered acceptable street attire, but thongs (flip flops) are not. During monsoon season, raincoats and umbrellas are necessary. Temperatures from January through March can be very cool, but you needn't bring heavy winter wear.

## Temple and Wedding Attire

Shorts should not be worn when visiting temples or shrines. Women may wear pants, but their tops must cover their shoulders.

Never wear white to a traditional Chinese wedding. It's a mourning color. (However, brides do wear white at Western-style marriage ceremonies.)

## Reading the Hong Kong Chinese

### Masters of Indirection

Understanding the dynamics of Chinese behavior is a major asset to foreigners, both in the business and social realms. Body language, subtle remarks, and patterns of conduct can tell you more about a situation than any verbal communication. Most Westerners value unambiguous dialogue, while Chinese value what is oblique or implied. What remains unspoken can be more important than what is said. Even seating arrangements can tell you how the Chinese view a meeting. Recognizing such nuances and knowing how to respond to them will both elicit respect and increase everyone's comfort.

### Gestures and Expressions

- The meaning of laughter or smiles among the Chinese depends on the situation. For example, when embarrassed or uncomfortable, Chinese will smile or laugh nervously and cover their mouths with their hands. This may be in response to an inconvenient request, a sensitive issue or an inadvertent mistake in behavior. Another example: Many Chinese believe that

spirits constantly hover overhead. If a bus driver should inadvertently close the door on a passenger, he might laugh to attract good spirits, since crying in dismay will attract evil ones to his bus.
- Holding one's hand up near the face and waving slightly means "no," or possibly a slight rebuke.
- When yawning, coughing, or using a toothpick, Chinese cover their mouths; a polite guest will follow suit.
- Hissing is a sign of difficulty or discomfort.
- To beckon someone, extend the arm palm downward and make a scratching motion with the fingers. Never curl your index finger toward you with the palm up. It is a gesture used only for animals.
- Many Chinese dislike having their photograph taken. An old Hakka and Hoklo superstition has it that preserving one's likeness on film steals the soul away.
- Unlike citizens in some other parts of Asia, Hong Kong Chinese do not remove their shoes when entering a home.

# 20 Entertaining: The Banquet Tradition

## China Invents the Restaurant

The first written mention of restaurants occurred in a second century B.C. Chinese document. A strategist by the name of Chia the First, tired of fending off the advances of the Hsiung-Nu (a troublesome enemy tribe), wrote to the emperor suggesting that eating establishments be built along the border. "When the Hsiung-Nui have developed a craving for our cooked rice, stews, roasted meats and wine," he wrote, "this will have become their fatal weakness." Ever since, the Chinese have tamed potential enemies with their culinary skills.

## Palaces Ablaze in the Night

Eating and business compete for first place as Hong Kong pastimes. You will rarely, if ever, be invited to a Chinese business associate's home for a meal, but you may very well be invited to a lavish, traditional banquet. These are held in restaurants with private rooms (usually upstairs) reserved for

# Entertaining: The Banquet Tradition

this purpose. If you like Chinese food, this may be the most pleasant part of your stay. (Peking duck or *pei ching*, served with thin pancakes, hoisin sauce and scallion "brushes," is a Hong Kong speciality.)

Business entertainment is, for the most part, a male domain. Wives are rarely invited. If you're a female executive, don't bring along your husband unless specifically invited to do so.

If the banquet is held on board one of the several floating restaurants in Aberdeen harbor, you're in for an additional treat. These gaudy palaces, three to five stories tall, are painted in scarlet, green and gold with fluted Chinese roofs. Images of gods, gargoyles and dragons guard their entrances. In the evening, they blaze with lights that reflect on the waters below.

## Using Chopsticks

Learning to use chopsticks before you arrive in Hong Kong is time well spent. (One way to practice is picking up peanuts. When you can pick up a bowlful of peanuts, one at a time, with relative ease, you should have no trouble at dinner.) If you absolutely cannot master the knack, silverware will be provided. This entails a slight loss of face, but it is preferable to making a mess by using chopsticks ineptly. With silverware, it's most appropriate to eat continental (European) style, with the fork remaining constantly in the left hand.

If you use chopsticks, here are some rules:

- Although it might seem a natural thing to do, it is extremely rude to stick chopsticks upright into a bowl of rice. (It reminds Chinese of the incense burned at funerals.)
- Never use chopsticks to point.
- When you are not using your chopsticks, put

them down on the chopstick rest provided, not on a bowl or plate.

## Banquet Etiquette

All the members of your party should arrive together and on time. You will be met at the door and escorted to the banquet room, where your hosts probably await you. Traditionally, the head of your team should enter the room first. Your hosts may applaud as you enter; accept this graciously. The proper response is to applaud in return.

Each round banquet table seats up to twelve people. If there are more than twelve, guests and hosts will be divided equally among tables. Seating arrangements are based on rank. The principal host sits farthest from the door facing the room entrance, usually with his back to the wall. The principal guest sits to the host's immediate right. Lower-ranking guests are seated in descending order around the tables, alternating with Hong Kong hosts. Never assume that you may sit where you please; your host will guide you to the appropriate place.

Each place setting includes a rice bowl, a main course dish, a dessert dish, a spoon, and chopsticks on a chopstick rest, usually with a napkin nearby. Two glasses are customary: a larger one for beer or soda and a small thin one for hard liquor. In the middle of the table is a circular revolving tray; during the meal, guests can spin it for access to any dish.

Banquet crockery may show chips and cracks and the linen may be slightly stained or mended. Chinese are more interested in food than its surroundings and are suspicious of eating establishments that waste money on decoration, tablecloths or candles. Chinese like to see what they eat, so the light may seem harsh to Western eyes.

# Entertaining: The Banquet Tradition

## Smoking and Drinking

You will probably be offered cigarettes throughout the banquet. (Lighting up without first offering a cigarette to others is considered rude.) You may decline without losing face, but unless you're severely allergic, bear with the secondhand smoke. Asking a host to refrain from smoking while enjoying a banquet is a terrible loss of face for both of you.

Beer is the standard banquet drink, along with brandy, cognac and tea (the latter breaks down the oil common to Cantonese and Pekinese food). You may also be offered *Mao-tai*, a wicked, 120 proof, sorghum-based wine. (Beware of toasting bouts in which you'll be expected to empty your glass in a single swallow.) Drinking liquor without eating, unless you are at a bar, is considered impolite.

Banquet drinking begins with the host's first toast. He will probably stand, hold his glass out with both hands and say a few words to welcome, concluding with *Yamsing* or *Gon booi* (Cantonese equivalents of "Cheers!"). At this, all present should drain their glasses. The head of the visiting group should respond with a toast to his host's well-being.

A courteous host will try to get his guests drunk. You can avoid this either by self-restraint (though you may be teased good-naturedly) or by claiming an allergy to alcohol. Many Asians cannot metabolize alcohol as quickly as Westerners; they tend to get drunk more quickly, and their faces may turn deep red.

## The Feast Begins

The first course in a banquet is an array of appetizers — such as pork, chicken, codfish, scallops, pickled vegetables and tofu (bean curd). Tasting each dish is polite, though not mandatory. Avoiding foods your body does not tolerate is preferable to gagging something down. If you find something on your plate you do not like, push it around to give the appearance that you've at least tried it.

At very formal banquets, people do not begin eating until the principal host has served a portion to the principal guest. The host may instead raise his chopsticks and announce that eating has begun. After this, feel free to serve yourself any amount, but avoid digging through a dish in search of the choicest morsels. You will not lose face by eating sparingly, but be aware that Chinese hosts appreciate guests with hearty appetites. Proper etiquette requires serving spoons or large chopsticks be used to transport food to a dish, but many Chinese use their eating chopsticks for this purpose. Watch your host and follow his lead.

Waiters will constantly replace dishes as they are emptied; keeping track of how much you've eaten and how much is yet to come (ten or twelve courses are common) is difficult. The second-to-last dish is often a sweet-and-sour one (possibly a whole fish). Tradition dictates that the penultimate dish be a delicacy procured at great expense, such as shark's fin soup.

Eat slowly. Stopping before the last course is considered bad form, and your host may think he has done something to offend you.

Don't expect Chinese fortune cookies at the end of the meal. They're a Western invention, the brainchild of a Japanese man who lived in San Francisco, California. (If you ask for them, you may be laughed at.)

# Entertaining: The Banquet Tradition

## Relaxed Manners

Table manners at Chinese banquets are unique. Elbows on the table indicate comfort; reaching across the table to serve yourself suggests the excellent quality of the food. Handle most food with chopsticks, but you may use your hands when eating chicken, shrimp, or other unwieldy items. Place bones and shells on the tablecloth; waiters will periodically rake this debris into a small bucket. Slurping and belching are considered signs of satisfaction.

## The Check

At the end of the meal, you will probably not see a check. If one comes, your host will pay it; and Hong Kong etiquette prohibits a guest from even suggesting that the bill be split. Accepting an invitation to dinner puts you in debt to your host. Repay the favor by inviting him out for a meal at a later date.

You can signal for the check in a restaurant by getting a waiter's attention and making a writing motion with your hands. Or you might ask for it in Cantonese: *"Maai dahn?"*

## A Note on Tipping

Some American restaurants and cafes have clever little signs by the cash register that read "Tipping is not a city in China." Neither is tipping a *custom* in China, having originated in the West. If you are a guest, permit your host to decide this issue. Fancy restaurants include a 10 percent service charge in your bill. If you're alone, let your conscience be your guide, but don't feel obliged to reward bad service.

## Socializing

Both Westerners and Asians work long hours in Hong Kong, and both need to "decompress" at the end of the day. Discretion is a necessary trait in the goldfish bowl of this crowded culture, so an informal rule has developed in the business community: When you live on the Hong Kong side, you play on the Kowloon side and vice versa.

Most Chinese people's philosophy of nightlife in Hong Kong is *hek, hot, woon, lok* — eating, drinking, playing and having fun. Regardless of cost, your host may insist on paying for everything as a matter of face.

### Karaoke: Star in Your Own Music Video

After dinner, Hong Kong Chinese may invite you to a karaoke club, a fairly recent import from Japan. (*Kara* means "empty" and *oke* is short for "orchestra.") Here, groups of (often inebriated) friends and business associates take turns singing popular songs to each other.

Karaoke clubs feature a raised platform with a standing microphone below a television monitor which displays pre-selected music videos that depict the song's story. The words are displayed at the bottom of the screen. Expect to be called upon to sing at least once. Ignorance of Chinese music will not save you; many clubs have American songs ("My Way" and "Yesterday" are very popular). Any attempt, no matter how poor, will be greeted with much praise and applause. In higher-class karaoke clubs, large private rooms are available; patrons can sing and drink until the sun comes up.

Karaoke singing is one of the very few socially acceptable ways in which an individual can display his or her talent without being branded arrogant or self-centered (and without jeopardizing the need to be accepted by the whole group). Participation in an evening's entertainment is an excellent way to establish close relations with the Hong Kong Chinese.

## Let It Ride

Gambling is a cultural phenomenon in China. Winning a wager means that the lucky person has chosen a number favored by the gods. Anything can be the focus of a bet, from sports to the weather.

Unfortunately, gambling is also strictly forbidden by the government (but available in nearby Macau). Its only legal form is at the Royal Hong Kong Jockey Club in Happy Valley. The ponies gallop from October until May, and the races are usually held at night. After taxes, some of the Jockey Club's profits are directed to the coffers of the government treasury, and the rest is distributed to charity. In 1995, these charitable contributions totalled over US$250 million.

## Mahjong

Mahjong appears to have originated in the late 19th century among boatmen on China's rivers. It was originally played with cards, but as these were likely to be blown overboard, they were replaced with small, rectangular blocks ("tiles") made of bone or ivory backed with bamboo. The name is a kind of onomatopoeia imitating the sound the tiles make during play. (*Mah* means "flax" or "hemp plant" and refers to the sound of leaves in the wind. *Jong* means "sparrow" and recalls the bird's chattering.)

Designed for two to four people, the game soon became popular in clubs in Canton and Shanghai, was introduced to Japan circa 1907 and to the United States after the First World War. As the game's stature grew, mahjong sets (144 tiles each) were sometimes crafted out of mother-of-pearl and even jade.

In modern-day Hong Kong, mahjong is both endemic and illegal (no one plays without betting), played mostly by the elderly and retired — and played at an astonishing speed. On any given evening, the sound of clicking tiles can be heard in homes and in the back rooms of restaurants throughout the colony.

Before joining Chinese friends or associates for a game, however, keep in mind that while mahjong is openly tolerated, gambling convictions carry severe punishments.

## La Scala, Hong Kong Style

Most nights, Chinese opera is performed at the Lai Chi Kok Amusement Park in Kowloon. Ticket prices are low — less than HK$20.

Cantonese opera (the form usually seen in Hong Kong) features beautiful costumes and headdresses, along with dramatic makeup. (Peking opera, though less colorful, has history on its side. It was performed before the emperors of China for centuries.) Stage props are considered unimportant; the audience is expected to visualize them. The orchestra is always on stage, and some of its music may seem loud and discordant to Western ears.

Though younger people prefer nightclubs and movies, the Chinese opera has been somewhat revitalized in recent years. Its performances are part of the annual Hong Kong Arts Festival, and there are regular appearances at the Arts Centre. The opera is an uncommon experience for the foreign visitor, but it's a splendid way to experience a little of Hong Kong's rich culture.

## Bar Hopping

Going to bars is a middle-management form of entertainment, and you should consider such an invitation as an acceptance of you as a peer. Hong Kong *tai-pans* prefer to make private arrangements for amusement, so you lose no face by not being invited.

If you don't drink, one solution is to explain that alcohol doesn't agree with you. If you empty a cup or glass, it will quickly be refilled. If you let it stay full, the only danger is that someone will bring you an additional glass and fill it.

## Fish, Birds and Butterflies

Ferry rides along Hong Kong's harbor, available both day and night, afford a spectacular view of the city for both visitors and locals. The Peak Tram, a true funicular, offers a panoramic aerial view.

Children are fond of Ocean Park, which features an immense aviary, a butterfly house and a new reef aquarium. To get there, take the breathtaking cablecar ride from Lowlands in Aberdeen.

## 22. Basic Cantonese Phrases

| English | Cantonese |
| --- | --- |
| Yes<br>No | *Hai*<br>*Mm hai* |
| Good morning<br>Hello (daytime)<br>Hello (evening)<br>Hello (telephone) | *Jo san*<br>*Neih hau*<br>*Maan ngon*<br>*Weyyy?* |
| Good-bye (colloquial) | *Joi geen* |
| Please | *Mm goi* |
| Thank you | *Doh je* |
| How may I address you? | *Dim ching foo nei a?* |
| Excuse me, I'm sorry | *Mm goi, dui mm jue* |
| My surname is _____ | *Sui sing* _____ |
| I don't understand | *Ngoh mm ming* |
| Do you speak English? | *Nei ssik gong ying man a?* |
| See you tomorrow | *Ting yat joi gin* |

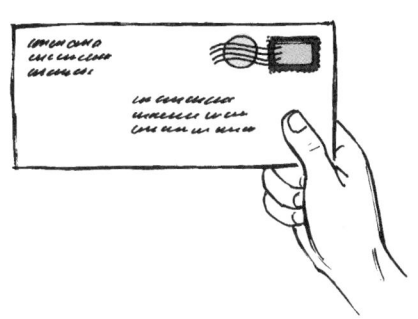

# 23 Correspondence

In general, a Chinese address written in Roman letters is the same as most Western addresses. For example:

Mr. WONG Yat-ming
International Publishing Ltd.
4/F, Island Building
31 Repulse Bay Road
CENTRAL
HONG KONG

The fifth line (CENTRAL) refers to the principal international business district of Hong Kong Island. The island's other districts are Aberdeen, Happy Valley and Taikoo Shing. (Hong Kong has no states or provinces, and there is no postal code system.) The last line of an address will read either Hong Kong, Kowloon or New Territories.

Although red is an auspicious color in Chinese culture, you should avoid using red ink, even when giving someone your address or phone number. It's considered a sign of unfriendliness.

# 24. Useful Numbers

These are local Hong Kong numbers. If dialing from outside Hong Kong, you must use your country's international access code and the Hong Kong country code [852]. Since 1995, all Hong Kong numbers are 8 digits. Old 7-digit numbers were converted by adding a "2" at the beginning.

- International Direct Dial Access................... 001
- Emergency...................................................... 999
- Operator assistance ........................................ 013
- Local directory assistance (English) ......... 1081
- Time and Weather........................................ 1852
- Ace Care Hire Service Ltd.................. 2893-0541
- Avis Rent A Car................................... 2890-6988
- Cathay Pacific Airways ...................... 2747-1888
- China Airlines..................................... 2868-2299
- Dragonair.............................................2590-1188
- FedEx..................................................... 2730-3333
- General Post Office ............................ 2523-1071
- HK Convention & Exhibition Centre. 2582-8888
- HK Trade Development Council ...... 2584-4333
- Intercontinental Care Hire Ltd.......... 2338-3689
- Police Hotline (non-emergency) ....... 2527-7177

# 25. Books & Internet Addresses

## Books

**A Borrowed Place: A History of Hong Kong**, by Frank Welsh. Kodansha America, New York, USA, 1993. The most recent authoritative history of this undemocratic, freedom-loving society. The last chapter deals with events since 1972.

**Travelers' Tales: Hong Kong,** edited by J. O'Reilly, L. Habegger and S. O'Reilly. . Travelers' Tales, Inc., San Francisco, California, USA, 1996. Diverse first-person accounts offer tantalizing insights into Hong Kong culture.

**Chinese Etiquette and Ethics in Business**, by Boye De Mente. NTC Business Books, Lincolnwood, Illinois, USA, 1989. A broad survey of morals and values pertinent to business interaction, mostly in mainland China.

**Culture Shock! Hong Kong**, by Betty Wei and Elizabeth Li. Graphic Arts Center Publishing Company, Portland, Oregon, USA. A humorous introduction to many of the initially incomprehensible facets of Hong Kong culture.

**Dealing with the Chinese**, by Scott D. Seligman. Warner Books, New York, USA, 1989. The author has extensive experience in mainland China and uses personal stories and examples to illustrate Chinese behavior.

## Internet Addresses

**Asia Trade Network**
　　http://www.TradeAsia.com/
**Doing Business in Hong Kong**
　　http://www.hk.super.net/~rlowe/bizhk/bhhome.html
**Hong Kong Economic and Trade Office**
　　http://www.hongkong.org/
**Hong Kong Internet Directory**
　　http://www.internet-directory.com/
**Hong Kong Online Guide**
　　http://www.hk.super.net/~webzone/hongkong.html
**Hong Kong Starting Points**
　　http://csclub.uwaterloo.ca/nckwan/hk/hongkong.html
**Hong Kong Trade Development Council**
　　http://www.tdc.org.hk/
**Hong Kong Travel Guide**
　　http://www.asia-
**Hong Kong Wonder Net (H.K. Tourist Association)**
　　http://www.hkta.org/
**WWW Servers in Hong Kong**
　　http://www.cuhk.hk/hkwww.html
**Usenet groups**
　　soc.culture.hongkong
　　rec.travel.asia

# HONG KONG Business

**The Portable Encyclopedia for Doing Business with Hong Kong**

Part of the World Trade Press Country Business Guide series. Details 25 key business topics including the economy, labor, demographics, industry reviews, import and export procedures, marketing, business law, taxation, financial institutions, business culture, trade fairs, opportunities, business travel, foreign investment, and important addresses. Concise, informative and unconditionally guaranteed.

**HONG KONG Business**
ISBN 0-9631864-7-7
305 pages, 26 chapters, charts, graphs, color maps, illustrations and comprehensive index.

---

### Other Country Business Guides

- ARGENTINA Business • AUSTRALIA Business
- CANADA Business • CHINA Business
- HONG KONG Business • JAPAN Business
- KOREA Business • MEXICO Business
- PHILIPPINES Business SINGAPORE Business
- TAIWAN Business • USA Business

**Available from your local bookseller or order direct.**

---

**WORLD TRADE PRESS®**
*Professional Books for International Trade*

1505 Fifth Avenue
San Rafael, California 94901 USA
Tel: (415) 454-9934, Fax: (415) 453-7980
e–mail: WorldPress@aol.com
USA Order Line: (800) 833-8586

## World Trade Press
# Passport to the World Series
### Your Pocket Guide to Business, Culture and Etiquette

These pragmatic, engaging paperbacks contain detailed information about a country's business practices, negotiating style, etiquette, government, work environment, social mores, view of foreigners and much more.

Discover a wealth of hard-to-find information to help you break through cultural barriers and ease any fears about doing business in countries around the globe.

Passport Books are attractively illustrated, easy to read, portable and short enough to digest in one sitting.

---

### Other Passport to the World Books

- Passport ARGENTINA • Passport BRAZIL
- Passport CHINA • Passport FRANCE
- Passport GERMANY • Passport INDIA
- Passport INDONESIA • Passport ISRAEL
- Passport ITALY • Passport JAPAN • Passport KOREA
- Passport MALAYSIA • Passport MEXICO
- Passport PHILIPPINES • Passport RUSSIA
- Passport SINGAPORE • Passport TAIWAN
- Passport THAILAND • Passport UNITED KINGDOM
- Passport USA • Passport VIETNAM

**Available from your local bookseller or order direct.**

---

### WORLD TRADE PRESS®
*Professional Books for International Trade*

1505 Fifth Avenue
San Rafael, California 94901 USA
Tel: (415) 454-9934, Fax: (415) 453-7980
e–mail: WorldPress@aol.com
USA Order Line: (800) 833-8586